THIS CANDLEWICK BIOGRAPHY BELONGS TO:

Skit-Scat Raggedy Cat

ELLA FITZGERALD

written by ROXANE ORGILL

illustrated by SEAN QUALLS

CANDLEWICK PRESS

For Amy Ehrlich
R. O.

For Ginger
S. Q.

First edition in this format 2013

The Library of Congress has cataloged the original hardcover edition as follows:
Orgill, Roxane.
Skit-scat raggedy cat : Ella Fitzgerald / Roxane Orgill ; illustrated by Sean Qualls. — 1st ed.
p. cm.
ISBN 978-0-7636-1733-2 (hardcover)

1. Fitzgerald, Ella — Juvenile literature. 2. Singers — United States — Biography — Juvenile literature.
3. Jazz musicians — United States — Biography — Juvenile literature. I. Qualls, Sean, ill. II. Title.
ML3930.F5O65 2010
782.42165092 — dc22
[B]   2009047407

ISBN 978-0-7636-6459-6 (reformatted hardcover)
ISBN 978-0-7636-6458-9 (reformatted paperback)

17 18 19 20 APS 10 9 8 7 6 5
Printed in Humen, Dongguan, China

This book was typeset in Kabel.
The illustrations were done in acrylic, pencil, and collage.

Candlewick Press
99 Dover Street
Somerville, Massachusetts 02144

visit us at www.candlewick.com

Table of Contents

CHAPTER
ONE

Ella cranked the handle on the phonograph, and the three Boswell Sisters crooned, with honey in their voices:

When I take my sugar to tea
All the girls are jealous of me . . .

Her mother, Tempie, sang along in her sweet, high voice, and Ella danced. Over and over they played the record. Ella's little sister, Frances, put the needle back at the beginning each time. They forgot the washing and ironing, forgot even supper until Tempie's boyfriend, Joe, came home, hungry.

'Cause I never take her where the gang goes
When I take my sugar to tea.

2

The song danced in Ella's feet all the way to Benjamin Franklin School on Waverly Street. She leaned against the red brick wall and sang:

I'm a rowdy dowdy that's me
She's a high hat baby that's she . . .

Ella's big hoop earrings jumped as she put out one foot and then the other and did a little dippee-do. Her schoolmates flocked to her like hungry pigeons, bobbing their heads to her sure beat.

So I never take her where the gang goes
When I take my sugar to tea.

Ella sent the song and the dance to her mother, who was pressing white shirts at the Silver Lining Laundry and counting the minutes till lunchtime. Tempie never had enough money, but she could always manage to scrape together seventy-five cents for a new record.

3

CHAPTER
TWO

Ella was thirteen. Her mouth was too big and her eyes were squinty. Ella was not pretty, but she could dance. She practiced outside the apartment on School Street with her friend Charlie. When they did the Susie Q around the corner on busy Morgan Street, people reached into their pockets for change—and folks did not have much change to spare in 1930 in Yonkers, New York! Toss a nickel on the sidewalk for Ella and Charlie.

Not just Ella; everybody was crazy for dancing. The jazz bands were stomping out tunes that made people want to *jump,* and music was everywhere, sailing out of windows and doorways from phonographs and radios. At night, you could switch on the radio and shuffle to "East St. Louis Toodle-Oo" coming from the Cotton Club in Harlem.

Harlem was forty-five minutes and a world away. New dances sprouted there faster than weeds in the sidewalk cracks. The bigger boys in Ella's neighborhood went, came back, and taught the latest steps to Ella, but it wasn't enough. She had to go see for herself.

Ella and Charlie put their nickels together and took the Number 1 trolley to the end of the line (five cents). They climbed aboard the *rumble-rumble* subway train (five cents more) to 125th Street, New York City. They pushed through the turnstile, clambered down the stairs, and there it was: Harlem, at their feet. Dancing feet. *Tap, tap, slide* to the Savoy Ballroom on Lenox Avenue.

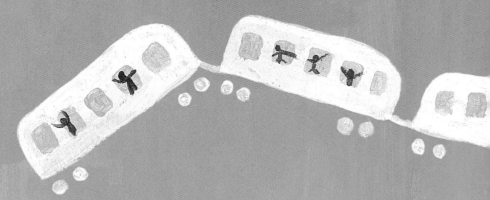

CHAPTER
THREE

The Savoy! Some people called it the "Home of Happy Feet." The polished dance floor was a block long, and the music never stopped, because there were two bands. As soon as one band took a break, the other kicked in, and so the dancing continued, on and on, all afternoon and into the night. Thirty cents got you in the door in the daytime. Ella watched and danced, listened and danced, and by the time the sun went down, she had the Lindy Hop *and* the Shorty George in her feet.

Now, when Ella and Charlie hopped the Lindy in Yonkers, people said good-bye to *all* their loose change. *Clink, plink, roll.* The kids were making more money than the shoeshine boys—"Three cents a shine!"

Ella and Charlie even got a few dancing jobs in clubs around the neighborhood.

Ella was going to be famous. She told everyone so. Never mind her broken-down shoes. Ella was raggedy and poor, but she was tough. All she needed was someone to notice her and give her a chance.

Instead she got a terrible blow.

Tempie died suddenly when Ella was fourteen. Ella was left with Joe, who didn't treat her kindly, so her aunt Virginia came to fetch Ella and bring her to live on 145th Street in Harlem.

Just like that, *wham shabam,* Ella lost everyone and everything she loved: first her mother, and then her home, her school, Charlie and her friends, and her dancing jobs.

Ella might have been happy in Harlem. She had her cousin Georgiana for company, and her sister, Frances, who came later. Ella might have been happy if her aunt Virginia had been able to give her some comfort and affection. But Virginia Williams offered meals and a roof, and nothing more.

CHAPTER
FOUR

Ella needed more. Ella was a rough-tough raggedy cat on the outside, but inside she was milky and silky and soft and shy.

The raggedy cat got rougher.

Ella started skipping school. When she wasn't keeping house for Aunt Virginia, she did things she shouldn't have: she ran errands for gambling men and did favors for people who were in trouble with the law.

Ella was hurting, and there was no one to notice. Ella broke the law herself once, twice, and then—

Skit-scat.

Ella got sent up the Hudson River to a school for orphans. It was an awful place, a nightmare place. They beat the girls, and the colored got it worse than the white. It was a regular routine to leave a girl alone in the basement, in chains, with nothing but bread and water to eat. The school was no place for a rowdy-dowdy high-hat baby with a broken heart. How could Ella dance in a nightmare? How could she sing with no one to send the song to?

Ella was tough. Somehow she endured the place for nearly two years and then—

Skit-scat skedaddle.

Ella ran away.

She went back to Harlem—not to her aunt's, where the police would find her and send her back up the river, but to Seventh Avenue.

Seventh Avenue! Where ladies in furs and men in checkered suits went to strut their stuff, especially on Sundays after church. Where the hoofers and tumblers, acrobats and comedy teams, jazz singers, jitterbugs, and the fabulous Edwards Sisters, the best kid dancers around, practiced their acts and collected the coins that people threw at their feet.

Ella danced the Big Apple and sang a little.

If her voice can bring
Ev'ry hope of the spring,
That's Judy!
That's Judy!

She had hooked the schoolkids in Yonkers with her singing; why not the fancy crowd in Harlem?

Ella tried to sound like Miss Connee Boswell. She tried to glide from note to note like a skater on ice, and put a little skip in the rhythm here and there.

If her eyes say "yes"
And you're wrong in your guess
That's Judy . . .

CHAPTER
FIVE

Where did Ella live? Anywhere and nowhere.
People took her in, gave her a meal and a bed.
Or didn't. In 1934, half of Harlem was out of
work. Men, women, and children were scrounging
in garbage cans for food. At the Baptist church,
you could get a bowl of soup for free. They gave
out used clothing, too. Ella got a pair of men's
boots to keep the cold off her dancing feet.

She was a half-starved raggedy cat of seven-
teen with no home, but she was free—free to
slip on down to the new Apollo Theater on 125th
Street as soon as she heard the news: the Apollo
had an Amateur Night on Wednesdays! You didn't
have to be famous—dancers, singers, anybody
could enter. The people in the audience were the
judges, and watch out: either they loved you or they
hated you, and they let you know it! First prize was
ten dollars and the chance to perform for a week with
the band.

To get on the program, Ella had to pass the Mon-
day audition, show her stuff to the emcee. She arrived
in a hand-me-down dress and her men's boots from the
Baptist church. Who should be ahead of her but the
Edwards Sisters, in sequined dresses and real dancing
pumps. The Edwards girls had pizazz and razzmatazz.
Ella couldn't dance after *them*! Her feet felt like bricks
in those clompy boots. She wanted to scram.

Her turn came, and she didn't dance. She sang
instead. Ella sang "Judy" and "The Object of My
Affection," and the emcee liked her enough to give
her a spot.

Showtime, 11 P.M., the Apollo Theater, November 21, 1934. Behind the crimson curtain, Ella was so nervous, her legs felt like water. She couldn't remember the words to her song, and she was the first amateur! What if they didn't like her?

Somehow she managed to push herself onto the stage, and then she started to sing off-key:

The object of my affection . . .

Her voice cracked.

The audience began to rumble. They had paid their thirty-five cents, and they wanted a show. "Boo, get that cat out o' there," someone shouted from the second balcony. In a moment a siren would shriek, and a man they called Porto Rico would come tearing out dressed like a skeleton or a hula girl or some other crazy thing. He would shoot his cap pistol and run Ella off the stage, while the audience howled.

Instead, the emcee stepped to the microphone and said, "Folks, hold on, now. This young lady's got a gift she'd like to share with us tonight. She's just having a little trouble getting it out of its wrapper. Let's give her a second chance."

This time Ella did not sing off-key, and her voice did not crack.

The object of my affection
Can change my complexion
From white to rosy red
Anytime he holds my hand
And tells me that he's mine.

Her voice was light and springy. Her beat was perfectly in time with the band. Soon even the noisemakers in the second balcony were holding on to every word. The feeling of being listened to—oh, it was a salve to Ella's sore heart.

When she finished, the audience hooted and hollered. The girl sounded just like Connee Boswell!

Ella won first prize.

CHAPTER
SIX

She got her ten dollars, but she didn't get her week with the band. You had to wear pretty clothes to sing in the regular shows. You had to be clean and presentable. Ella was a mess.

Somebody give that girl a bar of soap! A comb, a dress! But who? Ella had no home. She slept on a stranger's couch or a friend's dusty floor. She was a rough young thing with no thought for herself except this new desire: hang up those dancing boots and sing, you raggedy cat.

Ella gave it one more try. The Harlem Opera House had an Amateur Night, too. Again Ella was nervous, but this time she did not get lost in her song. She won first prize, and she got her week with the band, too.

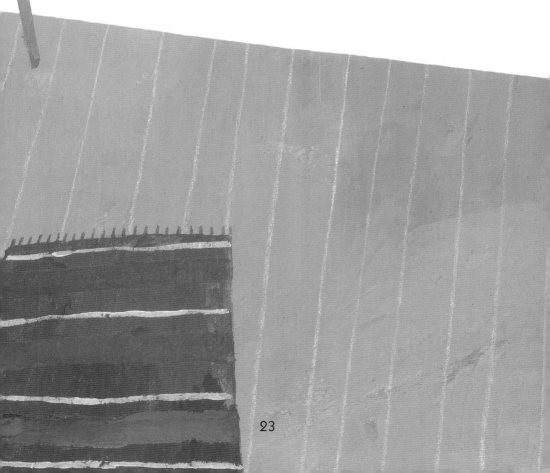

They put her on so late in the evening that people in the audience were putting on their coats and starting to leave. But then the bandleader announced, "Ladies and gentlemen, here is the young girl that has been winning all the contests," and Ella began to sing.

If her voice can bring
Ev'ry hope of the spring . . .

By the time she got to the end of the first line, people were taking off their coats and sitting down again. Soon their feet were tapping, and their shoulders were bobbing. Ella, too, was swinging with the beat, singing with her whole body.

If you're smart, watch your heart,
She'll upset 'most any fellow's apple-cart!

When the song ended, people jumped out of their seats, screaming and whistling. The noise— all for her! They liked her, oh! They liked her!

Folks were beginning to talk about Miss Ella Fitzgerald in Harlem.

CHAPTER
SEVEN

One day Ella was dancing and singing for tips on 125th Street—toss a coin in the can for Ella—when a stranger approached and said that Charles Linton from Chick Webb's band was looking for her. He needed a girl to sing the swing tunes, the fast numbers that sent people onto the dance floor.

Everybody knew Chick Webb. He had a drumroll like a burst of gunfire, and it made the dancers hop as if the floor were redhot. Well, all right, yes, Ella would give it a try. She walked over to the Opera House, where the Webb band was playing, to see what was what.

Mr. Linton was tall and slim and handsome. He wore a turban, and he was very popular with the ladies. When Ella sang "Judy" for him, her voice was small and shy.

"That's all right." said Mr. Linton. "Come on up, and I'll introduce you to Chick."

Chick Webb was a short man with a hump on his back. He took one look at Ella and said, "You're not puttin' that on my bandstand. No, no, no. Out!"

At the other end of the room, Ella wanted to flee. How could she sing for someone who didn't want to listen?

Sing for Tempie instead. She had been gone for three years now. Ella sent the song to her mother up in heaven.

> If she seems a saint
> And you find that she ain't,
> That's Judy, sure as you're born!

Chick Webb listened. He had wanted a pretty girl who could put across a song and make the band look good, but this raggedy cat had something else. She had a beat, a dancing beat he could feel in his drumming fingers. She might be just right for his hard-swinging band. Okay, he'd give her a tryout at the Savoy.

The Savoy, where Ella and Charlie had dropped thirty cents to learn the Lindy!

Chick's songs were all new to Ella, but she wrote the words on little cards, and by showtime, *ding a-ding a-ding,* she knew them by heart.

Somebody found her a dress, but oh, she was still a sight. "Hey, Sis, where'd you get those clothes?" the men in the band teased her. "Sis, what's with that hairdo?" Sandy the trombone player took her aside and gave her a bar of soap—told her to wash herself good. Helen, who looked after the costumes, took a comb to Ella's tangles every night.

But the dancers—the dancers couldn't get enough of her! Ella was not pretty, but so what? The girl could swing!

She'd had a dancing beat in her feet ever since she was a bitty girl in Yonkers, and all she ever needed was a chance to send that beat traveling up through her body, into her throat, and out her mouth in a song.

From his place behind the drums, Chick could see what was happening. Ella made people want to get up and *move.* He made her an official vocalist with the band.

CHAPTER
EIGHT

Ella had been singing and traveling with the
Chick Webb band for three years, and they were
the number-eight swing band in the *Down Beat* magazine
contest, but they still didn't have a hit song on the radio.

Ella had an idea for a song. It started with an old nursery rhyme.

A tisket, a tasket,
A—

Now, what color was that basket? She had to think back to when
she played drop-the-handkerchief with Charlie and her friends on
School Street.

A brown and yellow basket,
I sent a letter to my love —

No. She'd make it "mommie," for dear Tempie, gone to heaven.

I sent a letter to my mommie,
On the way I dropped it.

Ella wrote down the words as she remembered them, and then she
added a few of her own:

She was truckin' on down the avenue
With not a single thing to do,
She was peck, peck, pecking all around,
When she spied it on the ground. . . .

She took her words to Al, Chick's musical arranger, and he fooled
around on the piano until he found the right notes for the band to play.

A tisket, a tasket, a brown and yellow basket.

Every time Ella sang about her little basket, the dancers in the audience rushed to the stage to touch her outstretched hands or just the hem of her dress. They waved so many white handkerchiefs, it looked like washday at the Savoy.

Ella made a record of "A Tisket, A Tasket" with the band, and before you could say "a-little-girlie-picked-it-up-and-put-it-in-her-pocket," Ella and Chick had a number-one hit song on the radio.

ELLA FITZGERALD

Ella was twenty-one. She had a closet full of sparkly gowns with shoes to match and a wristwatch. She had a room at the Woodside Hotel on Seventh Avenue and a home with the Chick Webb Band, which was now tops in Harlem.

When Ella sang, people danced the night away. Sometimes they stopped and stood crowded shoulder to shoulder, in front of the bandstand, just to listen.

So long, Skit-Scat Raggedy Cat.

It's Rowdy-Dowdy High-Hat Baby now.

BIBLIOGRAPHY

FURTHER READING

Ella Fitzgerald: The Tale of a Vocal Virtuosa, by Andrea Davis Pinkney, illustrated by Brian Pinkney (Jump at the Sun, 2002), a picture book, tells Ella's story through the voice of a cat.

A-Tisket, A-Tasket, illustrated by Ora Eitan, is an artist's rendition of Ella's hit song (Philomel, 2003).

Ella Fitzgerald: A Biography of the First Lady of Jazz, by Stuart Nicholson (Routledge, 2004), is a biography for adult readers, with a discography by the indefatigable Phil Schaap.

The Ella Fitzgerald Companion, by Leslie Gourse (Schirmer Books, 1998), is a useful compendium of articles, reviews, and interviews, with brief, insightful commentaries by the author.

LISTENING

Before Ella Fitzgerald died in 1996 at age seventy-nine, she recorded more than 200 albums. Here are a very few:

Ella Fitzgerald with Chick Webb (Swingsation/GRP Records) contains the essential tunes they recorded from 1934 to 1939, the year of Chick's death, including "A Tisket, A Tasket."

Ella in Rome: The Birthday Concert (Verve) is Ella at her peak (age forty), and live.

Ella's eight "Song Books," renditions of songs by Cole Porter, George and Ira Gershwin, Jerome Kern, Harold Arlen, Rodgers and Hart, Johnny Mercer, Irving Berlin, and Duke Ellington, under the direction of Verve producer Norman Granz, are compiled in a sixteen-CD set, *The Complete Ella Fitzgerald*

Song Books (Verve). Choosing just one? *Ella Fitzgerald Sings the George and Ira Gershwin Song Book* is a gem, with arrangements by Nelson Riddle. Or sample them all in the single-CD compliation, *Ella Fitzgerald: The Best of the Song Books* (Verve).

Ella and Louis (Verve)—Louis Armstrong, of course—is a magical pairing. So is *Take Love Easy* (Pablo), duets with guitarist Joe Pass.

VIEWING

Ella Fitzgerald: Forever Ella, a "Biography" documentary (A&E Home Video, 2000), includes live performances and the last substantial interview with Ella.

Ella Fitzgerald: Something to Live For, an American Masters Documentary (Educational Broadcasting Corporation, 1999), includes lots of performance footage.

There are several concerts on DVD: try *Ella Fitzgerald—Live in '57 and '63,* in the Jazz Icons series (Tdk DVD, 2006).

ON THE WEB

The official website, www.ellafitzgerald.com, contains everything one needs to know.

The Ella Fitzgerald Charitable Foundation site, www.ellafitzgerald-foundation.org, is also recommended. The foundation was created and funded by Ella in 1993 "to use the fruits of her success to help people of all races, cultures, and beliefs," making donations to organizations whose concerns range from college scholarships to low-cost dental care, from after-school programs to diabetes research.

INDEX

ROXANE ORGILL is an award-winning writer on music and the author of several biographies for young readers, including *Footwork: The Story of Fred and Adele Astaire*, illustrated by Stéphane Jorisch, and *Mahalia: A Life in Gospel Music*, as well as a book for adults about music, race, and politics in the 1930s called *Dream Lucky*. Roxane Orgill lives with her husband and two children in New York City.

SEAN QUALLS is the illustrator of many books for children, including *Before John Was a Jazz Giant: A Song of John Coltrane* by Carole Boston Weatherford, for which Sean Qualls received a Coretta Scott King Honor for his illustrations; *The Poet Slave of Cuba* by Margarita Engel, winner of the 2008 Pura Belpré Award; *Dizzy* by Jonah Winter; and many others. Sean Qualls lives in New York with his wife and their two children.